Simon and Garfunkel

Bridge Over Troubled Water

Distributed by Music Sales Limited, 78 Newman Street, London W1P 3LA.

Cecilia

Words and Music by
PAUL SIMON

SUGGESTED REGISTRATIONS

General Electronic Organs		Drawbar Organs	
Upper:	Flute 16' 8' 4', Clarinet 8', Reed 8'	Upper:	44 8644 567
Lower:	Flute 8' 4', Diapason 8'	Lower:	(00)5655 432(0)
Pedal:	16' + 8'	Pedal:	5 - (3)
Vibrato:	On (Leslie: Tremolo)	Vibrato:	On (Leslie: Tremolo)

SUGGESTED DRUM RHYTHM: RHUMBA + BOSSA NOVA

With a strong beat ♩ = 104

Cel - ia, you're break-ing my heart, You're shak-ing my con - fi - dence

dai - ly,___ Oh, Ce - cil - ia, I'm down on my knees, I'm beg-ging you please to come

home, home, Ho ho home.___ Mak-ing love in the

Bridge Over Troubled Water

ENSEMBLE: GROUP BALLAD: BALLAD FLAUTIST
RHYTHM: 8 BEAT BALLAD
78

Words and Music by
PAUL SIMON

SUGGESTED REGISTRATIONS

General Electronic Organs

Upper: Flute 16′ 8′ 4′ 2′, Quint
Lower: Flute 8′ 4′, Diapason 8′
Pedal: 16′ + 8′
Vibrato: Off (Leslie: Chorale)

Drawbar Organs

Upper: 88 8800 008
Lower: (00)8876 000(0)
Pedal: 6–(4)
Vibrato: Off (Leslie: Chorale)

SUGGESTED DRUM RHYTHM: ROCK

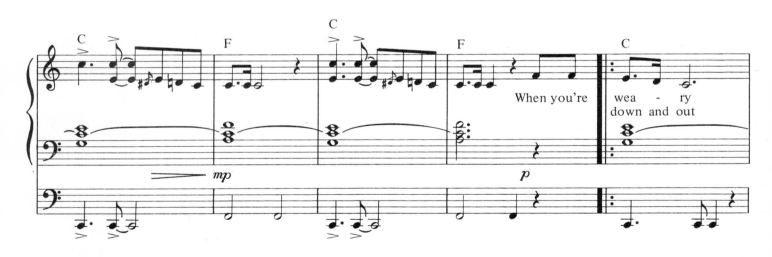

So Long, Frank Lloyd Wright

Words and Music by
PAUL SIMON

SUGGESTED REGISTRATIONS

General Electronic Organs

Upper: Flute 16′ 8′ 4′
Lower: Flute 8′ 4′, Diapason 8′
Pedal: 8′
Vibrato: Off (Leslie: Chorale)

Drawbar Organs

Upper: 80 7605 000
Lower: (00)8643 211(0)
Pedal: 4-(2)
Vibrato: Off (Leslie: Chorale)

SUGGESTED DRUM RHYTHM: BOSSA NOVA

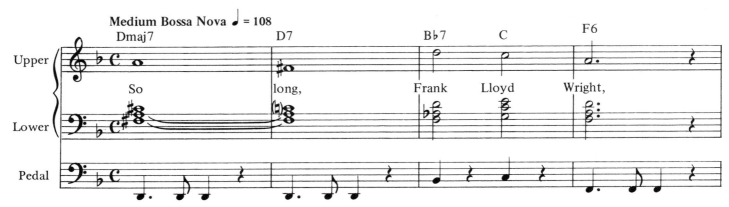

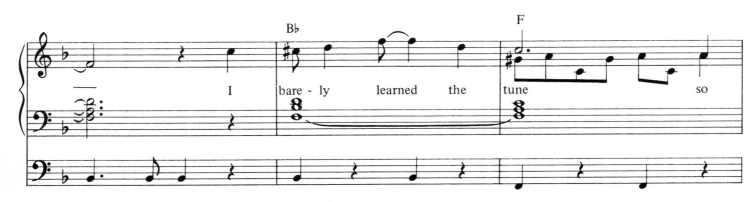

Keep The Customer Satisfied

Words and Music by
PAUL SIMON

SUGGESTED REGISTRATIONS

General Electronic Organs

Upper: Flute 16′ 8′ 4′, Trumpet 8′, String 8′
Lower: Flute 8′ 4′, Diapason 8′
Pedal: 16′ + 8′
Vibrato: On (Leslie: Tremolo)

Drawbar Organs

Upper: 73 6668 568
Lower: (00)6655 444(0)
Pedal: 5-(4)
Vibrato: On (Leslie: Tremolo)

SUGGESTED DRUM RHYTHM: SHUFFLE (OR MARCH §, OR SWING)

Why Don't You Write Me?

Words and Music by
PAUL SIMON

SUGGESTED REGISTRATIONS

General Electronic Organs	Drawbar Organs
Upper: Flute 16' 8' 4', Mixture 2', Quint	Upper: 85 8000 876 (+ 3rd Perc.)
Lower: Flute 8' 4', String 8'	Lower: (00)8800 000(0)
Pedal: 16' + 8'	Pedal: 6-(4)
Vibrato: On (Leslie: Tremolo)	Vibrato: On (Leslie: Tremolo)

SUGGESTED DRUM RHYTHM: ROCK

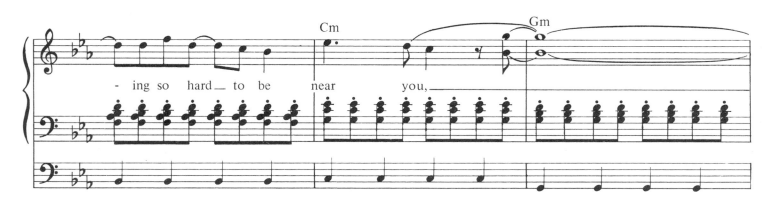

(Repeat and fade)

Baby Driver

Words and Music by
PAUL SIMON

SUGGESTED REGISTRATIONS

General Electronic Organs	Drawbar Organs
Upper: Flute 16' 8' 4' 2', Trumpet 8'	Upper: 88 8006 008
Lower: Flute 8' 4', Diapason 8'	Lower: (00)8833 442(0)
Pedal: 16' + 8'	Pedal: 5-(3)
Vibrato: On (Leslie: Tremolo)	Vibrato: On (Leslie: Tremolo)

SUGGESTED DRUM RHYTHM: SHUFFLE (OR MARCH $\frac{6}{8}$, OR SWING)

Bye Bye, Love

By FELICE BRYANT and
BOUDLEAUX BRYANT

SUGGESTED REGISTRATIONS

General Electronic Organs	Drawbar Organs
Upper: Flute 16' 4' 2'	Upper: 60 2804 815
Lower: Flute 8' 4'	Lower: (00)8733 300(0)
Pedal: 8'	Pedal: 5 – (2)
Vibrato: On (Leslie: Tremolo)	Vibrato: On (Leslie: Tremolo)

SUGGESTED DRUM RHYTHM: SWING

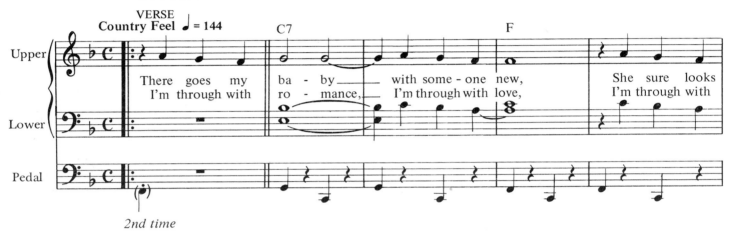

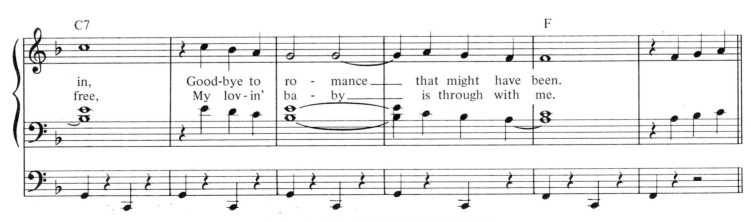

CHORUS

The Only Living Boy In New York

Words and Music by
PAUL SIMON

SUGGESTED REGISTRATIONS

General Electronic Organs	Drawbar Organs
Upper: Flute 8' 4', Trumpet 8	Upper: 00 8864 321
Lower: Flute 8', Diapason 8'	Lower: (00)5233 000(0)
Pedal: 8'	Pedal: 4-(3)
Vibrato: On (Leslie: Tremolo)	Vibrato: On (Leslie: Tremolo)

SUGGESTED DRUM RHYTHM: BOSSA NOVA

Song For The Asking

Words and Music by
PAUL SIMON

SUGGESTED REGISTRATIONS

General Electronic Organs

Upper: Flute 8' 4'
Lower: Flute 8' 4'
Pedal: 8'
Vibrato: On (Leslie: Tremolo)

Drawbar Organs

Upper: 00 7600 000
Lower: (00)6732 000(0)
Pedal: 4-(2)
Vibrato: On (Leslie: Tremolo)

SUGGESTED DRUM RHYTHM: WALTZ

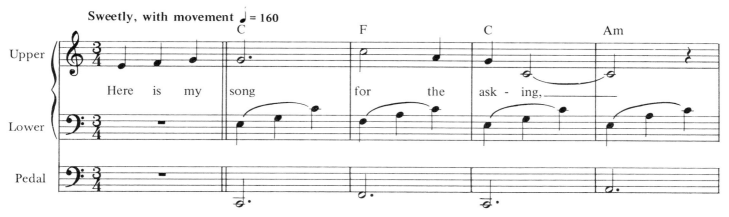

The Boxer

Words and Music by
PAUL SIMON

SUGGESTED REGISTRATIONS

General Electronic Organs

Upper: Flute 16' 4' 2'
Lower: Flute 8', String 8'
Pedal: 8'
Vibrato: On (Leslie: Tremolo)

Drawbar Organs

Upper: 60 2804 004
Lower: (00)7633 300
Pedal: 5-(3)
Vibrato: On (Leslie: Tremolo)

SUGGESTED DRUM RHYTHM: BOSSA NOVA

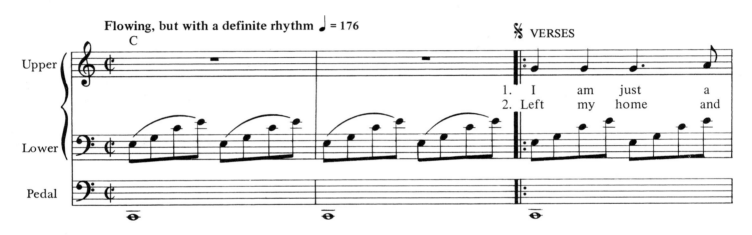

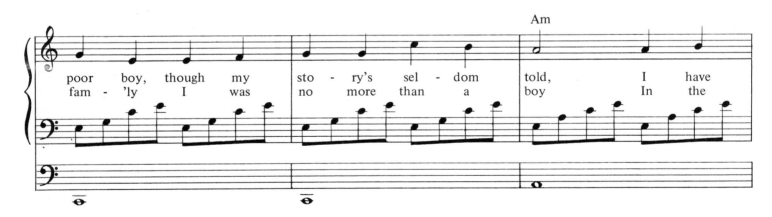

3. Asking only workman's wages I come looking for a job,
   But I get no offers
   Just a come-on from the whores on Seventh Avenue
   I do declare, there were times when I was so lonesome
          I took some comfort there,
   La la la la la la la

      Lie-la-le *(etc.)*

4. Then I'm laying out my winter clothes and wishing I was gone
   Going home
   Where the New York City winters aren't bleeding me
   Leading me, going home.

5. In the clearing stands a boxer, and a fighter by his trade
   And he carries the reminders of ev'ry glove that laid him down,
   Or cut him till he cried out in his anger and his shame:
   "I am leaving, I am leaving"
   But the fighter still remains

      Lie-la-lie *(etc.)*

      (Repeat and fade)

El Condor Pasa

Musical Arrangement by
J. MILCHBERG and D. ROBLES
English Lyric by
PAUL SIMON

SUGGESTED REGISTRATIONS

General Electronic Organs		Drawbar Organs	
Upper:	Clarinet 8', Oboe (Reed) 8'	Upper:	60 8866 666
Lower:	Flute 8' 4'	Lower:	(00)7655 432(0)
Pedal:	8'	Pedal:	4-(2)
Vibrato:	On (Leslie: Tremolo)	Vibrato:	On (Leslie: Tremolo)

SUGGESTED DRUM RHYTHM: RHUMBA + BOSSA NOVA

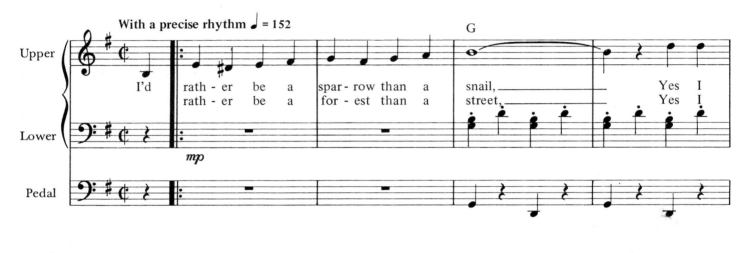

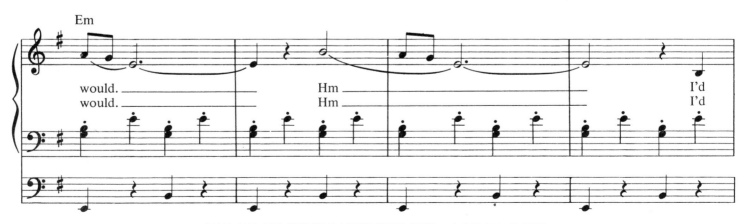

Printed in Great Britain by litho by The Anchor Press Ltd and bound by Wm Brendon & Son Ltd both of Tiptree, Essex